THE MUSEUM OF THE CITY OF NEW YORK
Portraits of America

The Empire State Building

THE MUSEUM OF THE CITY OF NEW YORK
Portraits of America

The Empire State Building

John S. Berman

BARNES
&NOBLE
BOOKS
NEW YORK

A BARNES & NOBLE BOOK

Library of Congress Cataloging-in-Publication Data

Berman, John S.
    The Empire State Building / John S. Berman.
        p. cm. — (Portraits of America)
    Includes bibliographical references and index.
    ISBN 0-7607-3889-0 (alk. paper)
    1. Empire State Building (New York, N.Y.)—History. 2. empire State
    Building (New
York, N.Y.)—Pictorial works. 3. New York (N.Y.)—Buildings, structures,
etc. I. Title. II.
Series.

    F128.8.E46 B47 2003
    974.7'1—dc21
                                                    2002038476

Editor: Betsy Beier
Art Director: Kevin Ullrich
Designer: Liz Trovato and Wendy Fields
Photography Editor: Lori Epstein
Digital Imaging: Daniel J. Rutkowski
Production Manager: Richela Fabian Morgan

Color separations by Bright Arts Graphics (S) Pte Ltd.
Printed in China by C&C Offset Printing Co. Ltd.

10 9 8 7 6 5 4 3 2 1

The publisher gratefully acknowledges the Skyscraper Museum
(skyscraper.org) for providing a number of photographs from their book
Building the Empire State (W.W. Norton, 1998).

About the Museum of the City of New York

The Museum of the City of New York is one of New York City's great cultural treasures—the first U.S. museum dedicated to the study of a single city. Founded in 1923, it presents the nearly four hundred–year evolution of one of history's most important metropolises through exhibitions, educational programs, and publications, and by collecting and preserving the artifacts that tell New York's remarkable stories.

The Museum's collection of 1.5 million objects reflects the diverse and dramatic history of New York City. In addition to prints and photographs, the Museum collects and preserves paintings and sculptures, costumes, theater memorabilia, decorative arts and furniture, police and fire fighting materials, toys made or used in New York, material related to the history of the port, and thousands of varied objects and documents that illuminate the lives of New Yorkers, past and present. Among the gems of the collections are gowns worn at George Washington's inaugural ball, New York's last surviving omnibus and one of its last Checker Cabs, archives of the work of renowned photographers Jacob A. Riis and Berenice Abbott, the world's largest collection of Currier & Ives prints, and pieces of the Times Square news "zipper."

Through its Department of Learning, the Museum offers programs to thousands of teachers and students from all five boroughs every year, including guided tours, teacher training, and its annual New York City History Day contest— the nation's largest urban history fair. Other activities for audiences of all ages include hands-on workshops, performances, book readings, scholarly conferences and lectures, films, and walking tours.

The Museum's rich collections and archives are available to the public for research. To learn how to explore the collections or how to order reproductions of images, visit the Museum's website at www.mcny.org. The website also features exhibition previews, up-to-date program information, an on-line Museum shop, virtual exhibitions, student aids, and information on how you can support the Museum's work.

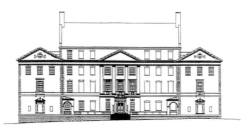

MUSEUM OF THE
CITY OF NEW YORK
1220 Fifth Avenue
New York, NY 10029
(212) 534-1672
www.mcny.org

Contents

Above: This aerial photograph beautifully captures the contours of the world's most famous skyscraper, especially highlighting the setbacks on the top and bottom floors and emphasizing the grace of the soaring tower.

The Eighth Wonder of the World

It is a painful irony that after September 11, 2001, the Empire State Building again stands as New York City's tallest building. It is ironic because for most New Yorkers who came of age prior to the 1970s, the Empire State Building epitomized both the city's grand skyline and its status as the birthplace of the American skyscraper. When the massive structure was completed in 1931, it seemed larger than life. Proclaimed the eighth great wonder of the world, it became a symbol of the city's grandeur and status even in the midst of the Great Depression. People from around the country and throughout the world flocked to the observation deck of the tallest building in the world to take in the thrilling view that stretched for miles and miles. In short, the 1,250-foot (381m)-high Empire State Building was the first thing many people thought of when they envisioned New York City.

Skyscrapers had been dotting the city's landscape for more than three decades prior to construction of the massive structure on the corner of 5th Avenue and 34th Street. Thanks to a huge influx of capital and new businesses, the island of Manhattan, always faced with a shortage of land, began to build "up" rather than "out" at the end of the nineteenth century. This phenomenon was made possible by technological advances, most notably the passenger elevator and steel-frame construction, which could support much taller buildings.

These new buildings seemed to fly up at breakneck speed; the eleven-story Tower Building went up in 1889, followed within a year by the eighteen-floor World Building. Fast on their heels came the triangular, twenty-one-story Flatiron Building, built in 1902. The 612-foot (186.5m)-tall, forty-seven-story Singer Building, however, completed in 1908, dwarfed all these structures, holding the title of world's tallest building for just one year, until the seven-hundred-foot (213.5m)-tall Metropolitan Life Building was constructed. The title changed hands again in 1913 with the construction of the Woolworth Building, which topped out at a towering 792 feet (241.5m). Even though more than one hundred skyscrapers sprouted up in Manhattan over the next two decades, former Governor Alfred E. Smith's August 1929 announcement about plans to build a new edifice, the scale of which had never been seen or even dreamed about anywhere in the world, still grabbed extraordinary attention.

As the massive economic boom of the 1920s turned into dust with the stock market crash of 1929, the construction of the Empire State Building took on new significance as a symbol of both defiance and hope. The building's audacious height and the remarkable speed with which it was erected seemed all the more impressive when juxtaposed against the economic despair of the city and the nation.

But the aura of the Empire State Building was always about more than the structure's height. It was also about a triumphant moment for architectural modernism and a style that later became known as Art Deco. In a discipline previously dominated by European sensibilities, American architects and designers were pioneering a movement for skyscraper design that was being recognized around the globe. Leaders in the field such as Harvey Wiley Corbett proclaimed skyscrapers to be America's gift to architecture, declaring that they represented the first new structural form since the invention of the arch by the ancient Romans. The Empire State Building, with its dizzying 102 stories, not only secured New York's place as a city of power and prestige, it also added to New York's reputation as the cultural standard-bearer for a country that was developing its own aesthetic style.

The way the Empire State Building was constructed, and how it was eventually used, also speaks volumes about New York City real estate development and New York City politics. For all the architectural grandeur of the building, it would not have been built at all without the efforts of speculator and General Motors executive John Jacob Raskob, or the desire of Al Smith to create a monument to his own historical legacy following his crushing loss to Herbert Hoover in the 1928 presidential election. The decidedly unromantic realities of power politics and shady real estate machinations also figured in decisions about who and what would occupy the many offices in the completed Empire State Building.

Not only did it attract more tourists than any other site in New York City, but the Empire State Building also gained special status as a pop-culture icon, becoming a favorite subject of photographers, filmmakers, popular magazines, and advertising campaigns. The best-known example was, of course, the movie *King Kong*, the climax of which involved a huge gorilla taking a captive Fay Wray to the top of the two-year-old Empire State Building, only to fall prey to her beauty. The plot, however, remains far less important than the fact that the star of the film may actually be the building itself. Other movies in which the building plays a prominent role include *An Affair to Remember*, *The Moon Is Blue*, and *Sleepless in Seattle*. It has also served as the starting point for the Great Atlantic Air Race from New York to London, and has been used as a venue for people attempting record-breaking feats, most notably those trying to scale the walls of the building from the outside.

The Empire State Building looms large in New York City history, not only because it has literally shaped the visual landscape, but also because its elegant tower has helped to define the very personality of the city in the modern era. From the audacity of its conception and the speed with which it was erected to the stylish figure it cuts in the Manhattan skyline, the Empire State Building has come to symbolize New York City itself.

Opposite: Visitors entering the 5th Avenue lobby are immediately struck by the dazzling ornamental panel of bronze and marble with a likeness of the Empire State Building, as well as medallions symbolizing the crafts and trades that went into the building's construction. Other wall panels display maps of New York and adjacent areas, with a gauge representing the direction in which the wind is blowing at the top of the building. The lobbies of all the entrances have colored marble floors, with Blue Belge marble for the borders set against a field of Red Levanto marble from Italy and Bois Jordan marble from France.

Above: An arch provides a dramatic frame for the Empire State Building in this view from the roof of the St. Gabriel's branch of the New York Public Library, which stood at 36th Street between 1st and 2nd Avenues.

Right: Visitors on top of the world at the 102nd floor observation deck. It is no longer possible for the general public to go beyond the 86th floor, although private parties that reserve in advance can obtain special permission to ascend up the additional sixteen floors.

Left: Al Smith chose to build the world's tallest skyscraper at 34th Street and 5th Avenue in part because of the site's proximity to first-class department stores, including B. Altman, Tiffany and Company, Lord and Taylor, Gimbel's, Saks, and, of course, Macy's, the world's largest department store, located just one block away on Herald Square.

Right: From the beginning, the Empire State Building served as a backdrop to the everyday life of the city. Here, a group of young men play baseball as the el passes by.

Opposite: For many New Yorkers, the Empire State Building is a familiar part of daily life in Manhattan, as this photograph from Madison Square Park, south of the skyscraper, makes clear.

Right: The Empire State Building appears to tower above the clouds themselves. It certainly helped the builders that the land on which the skyscraper was constructed was considerably higher than the surrounding area.

Right: This aerial view looking south makes the two high-rise worlds of Midtown, in the foreground, and Lower Manhattan, in the background, look like two competing cities.

Above: The Manhattan of the 1920s saw the birth of the skyscraper, with buildings reaching ever higher. The primary owner of the Empire State Building, John Jacob Raskob of General Motors, was determined to build a skyscraper taller than that of his adversary, Walter Chrysler.

CHAPTER ONE

Scraping the Sky

Although the century of the skyscraper was well under way by the 1920s, it was in this decade that the building boom in Manhattan hit its pinnacle. Beginning in 1923 and stretching until 1929, the amount of office space in New York City nearly doubled, and the growing metropolis witnessed the construction of more than fifty buildings that were at least thirty-five stories high. These structures included the Chanin, Lincoln, Daily News, and Chrysler Buildings in Midtown Manhattan, and the Irving Trust, Manhattan Company, and City Bank Farmers Trust Buildings in the burgeoning financial district.

By the 1920s, construction had become the second-largest industry in the nation, and in New York City the real estate boom created a massive feeding frenzy with assessed land values increasing an average of almost 13 percent each year. Both the city's industrial and service sectors were expanding by leaps and bounds. And each new business required office space, and often desired room to house an entire corporate headquarters. Bigger and taller, grander and higher, slimmer and sleeker—these seemed to be the mottoes for each new structure planned during the roaring twenties, and although New York was at the forefront, skyscrapers began adorning the landscape of cities such as Chicago, Philadelphia, and Detroit as well.

Although construction took place on a massive scale throughout the decade, 1929—the year that would end with the country mired in the Depression—saw the planning of the largest and most expensive buildings yet. In the first nine months of the year, more than seven hundred buildings were already on the drawing board at a total cost of nearly $500 million. By the spring of 1929, Manhattan was home to fifteen buildings more than five hundred feet (152.5m) high.

But not everyone was enamored with the proliferation of skyscrapers sprouting up around the city. Critics complained that Manhattan was becoming, in the words of housing reformer Lawrence Veiller, a "sunless city," and many advocated restricting the height of buildings to a maximum of ten stories. Although a movement to set new standards for skyscraper development was gaining ground, most attempts at restriction or regulation failed. A core group of influential New Yorkers viewed the tall towers as emblematic of American ingenuity and leadership in the twentieth century.

Nothing symbolized the seemingly endless race to build ever higher than the frantic competition to create the tallest structure in New York City. The challenge pitted William Van Alen's design for the new Chrysler headquarters on Lexington Avenue and 42nd Street against H. Craig Severance's Gothic-inspired building for the Bank of Manhattan at 40 Wall Street. Throughout the spring and into the

Right: An architect's rendering of the Empire State Building and the new Waldorf-Astoria Hotel, which had relocated to Park Avenue between 50th and 51st Streets. The original Waldorf-Astoria stood on the 34th Street site of the Empire State Building.

Empire State and Twin Towers of Waldorf Astoria Hotel, New York.

summer of 1929, New Yorkers craned their necks to watch the battle of the two skyscrapers, which were just four miles (6.4km) apart. By September of that year, the completed Bank of Manhattan Building appeared to emerge victorious as the tallest building in New York at 927 feet (282.5m), capped off by a fifty-foot (15m) flagpole. But on October 16, just thirteen days before Black Tuesday, Van Alen added a finishing touch to the top of the Chrysler Building: a majestic 185-foot (56.5m)-high steel spire that raised the new structure to 1,046 feet (319m) above street level. Van Alen's masterpiece now towered 119 feet (35.5m) higher than its neighbor to the south; it was now the tallest tower not only in New York City, but in the world.

In addition to being the world's tallest building, the Chrysler Building represented a triumph in at least three other respects. It stood as the foremost example of the new architectural style that came to be known as Art Deco, and it marked the eclipse of Midtown over Lower Manhattan as the island's frontier in commercial development. It also represented a huge feather in the cap of Walter Chrysler, who reigned over the most talked about physical structure in the world— an edifice that symbolized the power of the Chrysler Corporation in the emerging automobile age.

Chrysler would later discover that he had a major competitor more powerful than the Bank of Manhattan in John Jacob Raskob. A former General Motors executive, Raskob had bottomless coffers as well as strong political connections, both a result of having served as chairman of the national Democratic party and having managed former New York governor Al Smith's recent campaign for president. While the city was watching the Chrysler Building and the Bank of Manhattan Building rise, Raskob was planning to develop a site south of Midtown Manhattan, and he chose Al Smith, a much-beloved figure in New York City government, to be the president and chief spokesman for the project. The new building, announced by Smith on August 29, 1929, would sit on a two-acre (0.8ha) lot at the corner of 34th Street and 5th Avenue, the site of the former Waldorf-Astoria Hotel. In his typically flamboyant fashion, Smith announced that the new Empire State Building would be eighty-five stories—1,050 feet (320m)—high with more than two million square feet (186,000m²) of office space.

And yet, business-wise, the development of the Empire State Building was based entirely on speculation: unlike Chrysler, Raskob and Smith had not secured a single tenant to rent space in their enormous office complex. The location at 5th Avenue and 34th Street generated little, if any, interest among most commercial developers. It was in neither of the existing Midtown or Lower Manhattan office districts, nor was it convenient to rail or subway lines—important factors that contributed to considerable skepticism among critics. *Fortune* magazine commented: "If the owners are right, they may fix the center of the metropolis. If they are wrong, they will have the hooting of the experts in their ears for the rest of their lives."

Nevertheless, Raskob and his backers were anticipating a shift in the 5th Avenue corridor from a primarily residential area to an increasingly commercial one. Midtown Manhattan was in flux: the new 8th Avenue and 6th Avenue subway lines now connected Midtown to the outer boroughs, and a growing number of suburban commuters were making their way into the city by car and rail from New Jersey and Long Island. The area was under pressure to expand its available commercial real estate to meet this demand or risk being overlooked. For developers and builders in this era, even the sky was no longer the limit. And why should it have been? Land values and real estate prices in the area had continued to skyrocket throughout the 1920s. As a result, the owners of the Waldorf-Astoria Hotel had decided to reap a windfall by selling their building to the Bethlehem Engineering Company for approximately $16 million, a staggering profit, in December 1928.

MONARCHS of NEW YORK CITY

Chrysler Building

R.C.A. Building

Empire State Building

16366

Left: Postcards depicting New York City's famous skyscrapers reflected a push by public relations specialists in both government and the private sector to market these buildings as tourist attractions and to use them as major revenue sources for the city.

Right: This design sketch juxtaposes architectural renderings of the Empire State Building, the Eiffel Tower—which until 1930 was the world's tallest structure—and the Chrysler Building.

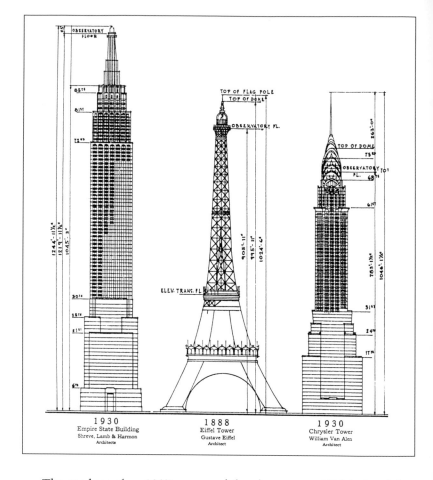

1930
Empire State Building
Shreve, Lamb & Harmon
Architects

1888
Eiffel Tower
Gustave Eiffel
Architect

1930
Chrysler Tower
William Van Alen
Architect

The product of an 1897 merger of the eleven-story Waldorf and the sixteen-story Astoria, the once proud Waldorf-Astoria Hotel had seen its social cachet fade over the preceding decade. So the owners decided to attempt to revive its popularity at a new site just north of Grand Central Terminal at Park Avenue between 50th and 51st Streets. Bethlehem's intention was to build a fifty-story mixed-use structure on the 34th Street site, an idea that was nipped in the bud when the company defaulted on its second payment in late April 1929 and was bought out by Phillip Kaufman, the president of Chatham and Phenix National Bank and Trust. That summer Kaufman appointed Raskob and Pierre DuPont as his principal stockholders. From the beginning of his involvement, Raskob pushed for the original fifty-story concept to be transformed into what would be a prestigious, "Class A" office tower. A more ambitious building of seventy or even eighty stories, he believed, would not only generate enormous publicity, but could raise as much as $1 million in additional rents. It was not until Smith's announcement in August, however, that the idea of erecting the largest building in the world was formally hatched.

It is unlikely that either Smith or Raskob could ever have imagined that in the very same month that the old Waldorf-Astoria was demolished to make room for the Empire State Building, the bottom would drop out of the stock market, plunging the nation into a severe depression—a depression fueled in part by the same real estate speculation frenzy that had made the site available in the first place. Undoubtedly, observers must have wondered if plans for the massive tower would be scaled back or even abandoned. They received their answer a scant six weeks after the stock market crash.

The Empire State Building would not only proceed as planned, it would be even taller and grander, with a two-hundred-foot (61m) tower that would raise the building to 1,250 feet (381m)—more than two hundred feet (61m) higher than the rival Chrysler Building. To add an additional twist to these grandiose plans, Smith announced that, unlike the Chrysler Building, the Empire State Building's tower

Left: The Waldorf-Astoria Hotel, the former occupant of the Empire State Building site, was the city's largest and most prestigious hotel. By the late 1920s, however, the grande dame of luxury hotels had begun to lose its luster, and the owners opted to sell the property. The old hotel was demolished in 1929 to make room for the Empire State Building and a new Waldorf-Astoria was built at a fashionable Park Avenue location.

THE FOUR PACEMAKERS

In considering the factor of speed, it is interesting to study the progress of those four divisions of the construction work which had to take the lead and set the pace for other trades that followed.

These four leaders in the order of their sequence were:

1. Structural Steel Erection
2. Concrete Floor Arch Construction
3. Exterior Metal Trim and Aluminum Spandrels (including metal windows)
4. Exterior Limestone (exterior trim and limestone backed up with common brick)

Structural Steel:

The structural steel for the eighty-five stories of the Main Building was topped out on September 19th, 1930 and completely set on September 22,1930.

The progress schedule called for completion of the steel on Oct.4,1930.

The time gained was twelve days.

Concrete Floor Arch Construction:

The floors for 85 stories including the Main Roof at the 86th floor level were completely poured on October 6, 1930.

The progress schedule called for completion of floor arches on Oct.10,1930.

The time gained was four days.

Exterior Metal Trim and Cast Aluminum Spandrels:

This work for the 85 stories was completely erected on October 17,1930. The progress schedule set Dec. 1,1930 as the completion date. The time-saving effected was 35 days.

Exterior Limestone (Including Common Brick Backup):

The 85 stories were completely enclosed on Nov.13,1930 ; a gain of 17 days over the schedule completion date of Dec.1,1930.

Revision of Progress Schedule:

The impetus gained by the various other trades following closely on the trail of the four leaders mentioned above, permitted a change to be made in the progress schedule. The original progress schedule called for completion of the construction work on April 1, 1931 in order to allow tenants to move in and start occupancy on May 1, 1931. The success achieved in being able to completely enclose the building before the advent of severe weather, permitted the final completion date to be advanced one month to March 1, 1931.

would be more than ornamental. It would serve as mooring mast for dirigibles (airships), which, on transatlantic routes, would dock in the sky over 34th Street and 5th Avenue. Passengers would then be whisked through immigration and customs inside the building.

The dirigible idea met with considerable skepticism among experts, and after several failed attempts to dock an airship, the plan was abandoned as impractical. But the public's imagination had nonetheless been sparked by a vision of the city's tallest structure operating as a port of entry for airships from around the world. It is also likely that neither Smith nor Raskob, nor many other New Yorkers, believed the economic downturn would last, and there seemed to be no reason not to continue to think big. President Herbert Hoover declared prosperity to be "just around the corner" and many Americans believed him. On January 22, 1930, under the direction of the architectural firm of Shreve, Lamb, and Harmon Associates and general contractor Starrett Brothers and Eken, workers began laying the foundation of the Empire State Building. The massive project was under way.

Opposite: General contractors Starrett Brothers and Eken made meticulous notes about all aspects of the construction process, and eventually compiled these records into a single notebook, one page of which is reproduced here. Only recently rediscovered, this notebook was made available to the public for the first time in *Building the Empire State* (W.W. Norton).

Above: Because the Empire State Building was the third structure to occupy the site, excavations required the removal not only of earth and rock, but also of the remains of old masonry and foundations. This March 21,1930, photograph shows the excavation nearly completed.

Opposite: The world's most famous skyscraper dwarfed the buildings that surrounded it in the 1930s.

Right: Here, the Empire State Building appears to stand alone in the night sky. As splendid as the building is under natural light, there is something transcendent about the skyscraper after dusk—truly a symbol for the city that never sleeps.

Right: Not everything connected to the old Waldorf-Astoria Hotel was destroyed prior to construction of the Empire State Building. Building contractors salvaged four elevators from the former hotel, including the one shown here. They were used to provide slower local service while the new skyscraper was in the initial stages of construction. This elevator ran to the 20th floor and was manufactured by A.B. See.

Opposite: Even though the outside of the Empire State Building has received the lion's share of the praise, the ornate, marble-adorned main lobby is one of its most striking features. The design incorporated a number of imported colored marbles: two colors from Germany, two from Belgium, two from Italy, and two from France.

Above: Former governor Alfred E. Smith presides over the cornerstone-laying ceremony in September 1930, after seventy-five stories of the structure's steel framework had been completed. A former bricklayer, Al Smith served as the "front man" and chief political backer of the massive skyscraper, which was in many ways his brainchild.

CHAPTER TWO

A Spectacular Gesture

As early as September 1929, John Jacob Raskob had directed the Empire State Building architects to have the new structure completed by May 1, 1931—an extraordinarily tight turnaround time that reflected his desire to bring tenants, and therefore income, into the building as soon as possible. In Shreve, Lamb, and Harmon, he had chosen the architectural firm responsible for creating many of Manhattan's skyscrapers, including the headquarters for Raskob's General Motors. Starrett Brothers and Eken were the city's industry leaders in erecting high-rises, including the forty-story New York Life Insurance head-quarters and the thirty-six-story McGraw-Hill Building. As part of their bid for the project, the firm also agreed to demolish the old Waldorf-Astoria and finish the Empire State Building in eighteen months.

The architects responded to the need for expediency by creating a simple, straightforward design with no cornices to cast shadows and no other conventional ornamental flourishes to mar the soaring lines. It is likely that the building's modern, functionalist style, which ensured maximum utility and efficiency of space, had as much to do with the needs of potential tenants and the financial imperatives of the moment as it did with the impulses of avant-garde architecture. At any rate, the final design was the result of the desire to create a space that was bright and airy—especially on the upper floors—and to imbue the skyscraper with character through the use of light and shadow, rather than through excessive architectural ornamentation.

In order to meet Raskob's deadline for completion, Lamb, working closely with Starrett Brothers and Eken, designed the elements of the structure—from the frame to the facade—with maximum construction efficiency in mind. Lamb made sure that most of the handwork was eliminated, allowing windows, spandrels, steel mullions, and stone to be replicated, "standardized," and then brought to the building site ready for assembly. The pieces were designed to fit together almost like a three-dimensional jigsaw puzzle, and the entire structure was erected assembly-line style, almost like one of Ford's automobiles. If suppliers could not deliver materials on time, new suppliers were quickly brought in. To save time, designers instructed draftsmen to make drawings for each floor as the floor below it was completed, and each activity was carefully synchronized so that all aspects of the work could proceed simultaneously.

Perhaps the most amazing thing about the building that became known for the boldness of its innovative form and design was the consistently pragmatic approach taken by the architects and builders. Whether it was the steel girders from Pittsburgh, the cement and mortar from upstate New York, or the Italian, French, and Belgian marble,

Right: Architects Richmond Shreve (whose first name was captioned erroneously on this image from a 1931 book) and William Lamb were considered pioneers in developing skyscrapers. They had been responsible for a number of the city's highest structures, including the New York headquarters for General Motors at 241 West 57th Street, the Standard Oil Building at 26 Broadway, and the National Lefcourt Building at 521 5th Avenue. Arthur Harmon joined the firm in 1929 and helped design the Salmon Tower at 500 5th Avenue.

ROBERT H. SHREVE

WILLIAM F. LAMB

ARTHUR LOOMIS HARMON

the delivery of materials from these disparate locales was closely coordinated to ensure that everything arrived ready to assemble, with a minimum amount of work required on site. Steel frames, columns, and beams, for example, arrived ready to be lifted into place and riveted into the previously assembled surrounding parts. "When we were in full swing going up the main tower," Shreve commented, "things clicked with such precision that once we erected fourteen and a half floors in ten working days." The machine-like efficiency of the construction and the innovative containment of costs became a source of great pride to the architects, as if the elegance of the structure were a direct result of the synchronicity, organization, and speed necessary to complete the project. At a time when the automobile industry had perfected the assembly line for manufacturing cars, Starrett Brothers and Eken had figured out how to utilize the same technique to erect a skyscraper.

Expense was also a major factor in deciding which materials would be used in the construction of the building. One good example is the sleek Indiana limestone adorning the facade of the building. Now celebrated for its beauty, the limestone was actually selected because it cost less than comparable stone. Likewise, the Empire State Building was the first skyscraper to use chrome-nickel steel fencing on its exterior. The use of this high-quality metal on the building's face meant that the exterior stonework could be minimized. The result is a very low ratio of stone volume to building volume—only one cubic foot ($0.03m^3$) of stone for every forty-five to fifty cubic feet ($1.3m^3$–$1.4m^3$) of space—an architectural innovation regarded as revolutionary, though it was also implemented as a cost-saving measure.

With all their collaborative organization, teamwork, and scientific management efforts, the builders and designers still needed the workers—thousands of workers—to accomplish the job. They included iron- and steelworkers, pipe fitters, cement finishers, stonecutters, elevator constructors, riveters, and engineers of all kinds. At the peak of the labor effort in August of 1930, there were 3,439 men employed at the site. Although Al Smith liked to boast that all the work on the building was accomplished by day, he was stretching the truth. Empire State Building laborers began their workday at 3:30 A.M., while the rest of the city was sound asleep, and finished at 4:30 in the afternoon. And, with the kickoff of the Great Depression, their wages were at rock bottom. For working these grueling, thirteen-hour days—with half an hour off for lunch—they were usually paid less than two dollars an hour.

Unlike other construction workers, who generally toiled in obscurity, laborers on the Empire State Building gained a public face if not an identity through the evocative documentary photographs of Lewis Wickes Hine, hired to chronicle the project's progress by Al Smith's longtime second in command, Belle Moskowitz. Although Hine had been known as a photojournalist who exposed the horrors of child labor, in this case he was hired mainly to call attention to the building itself, rather than to engage in commentary about working conditions on the site.

In fact, although six workers were killed in the construction of the Empire State Building, safety on site was generally at a high level. Nonetheless, Hine's photographs graphically document the dangerous nature of the jobs and the extreme difficulty of the work, especially for the riveters, who worked in teams of four joining the steel framework together one piece at a time while balancing on narrow beams one thousand feet (305m) or more in the air. Large crowds of onlookers would gather outside the construction site every day, standing awestruck as they watched the teams of riveters at work. The *London Daily Herald* even described these steel-nerved laborers as "classical heroes in the flesh." Sadly though, the country's descent into the Great Depression meant that many of the workers who built the tallest edifice in the world had little to look forward to other than unemployment.

Construction continued at a fervent pace through the summer and fall of 1930. By October, workers had completed the building's eighty-five-story main shaft and all that remained were the tower's upper beams, which were riveted into place during the bitterly cold and windy winter. By mid-March, the mooring mast was successfully constructed, and only a few weeks later, the finishing touches on the interior had been completed. The Empire State Building had not only been built on schedule, it had actually been finished ahead of schedule. Workers had erected nearly sixty thousand tons (54,420t) of structural steel in the sky faster than anyone could have ever dreamed; it rose at a rate of four and a half stories per week.

Al Smith positively beamed as he presided over the opening day gala on May 1, 1931. If the former governor was looking for a lasting legacy to wash away the bitterness of his crushing defeat for president, he received it in the completed Empire State Building, which the *Brooklyn Eagle* referred to as "the House that Smith built." Governor Franklin D. Roosevelt, Raskob and his partners, and the increasingly besieged New York City mayor Jimmy Walker (too busy battling myriad corruption charges to have had any direct involvement in the Empire State Building) joined Smith at the celebration. That evening, President Herbert Hoover pushed a ceremonial button in the White House that illuminated the interior of the massive building for the first time.

Right: On September 17, 1930, only one year after the signing of the first building contracts, Al Smith presided over the Empire State Building's cornerstone-laying ceremony.

Above: Construction workers (right) wait in line to collect their paychecks. Weekly wages were paid on site and the total payroll could be as high as $250,000 a day during weeks of peak employment. As a result, armed guards, shown here on the left, were hired to protect the money and to ensure that workers received their due.

Right: The Empire State Building's foundation columns are set on concrete piers that are sunk thirty feet (9m) below street level. The workers in the background look tiny compared to the massive steel pylons.

Right: On a typical day at the site, men worked together like a well-oiled machine, thanks to the efficient organization of every aspect of the construction. The general contractors on the project, Starrett Brothers and Eken, were chosen in large part because of their proven ability to manage complex projects and maintain tight construction schedules without compromising a building's design. Bill Starrett explained his philosophy in these terms: "The principal function of the general contractor is not to erect steel, brick, or concrete but to provide a skillful, centralized management for coordinating the various trades, timing their installations and synchronizing their work according to a predetermined plan."

Below and opposite: When construction on the Empire State Building began in 1930, noted photographer Lewis Wickes Hine was commissioned to document each phase of the process. Unlike most of his other assignments, in which he was brought in to uncover and document the abuse of working people, the Empire State Building project was intended to generate positive publicity for the building. Here, Hine portrays a worker bolting together a portion of the framework of the building (below) and men completing the skeleton of the mooring mast (opposite).

Right, top: Unlike most work sites, employees laboring on the Empire State Building were required to remain on site during their lunch breaks. From the point of view of building management, there were simply too many workers on staff to enable them all to descend down the elevator at the same time, leave the building, and then get back up the elevator on time for their afternoon shifts. As a result, several food concessions were provided. The one shown here was located on the third floor.

Right, bottom: One of the most important construction jobs was performed by the riveters, who worked in teams to fasten together the steel girders and columns used in the building. The process is shown here in a photograph by Charles Rivers, an iron-worker at the site. The extreme measures taken to speed the construction process required that each piece of steel be custom designed for a specific location. The *London Daily Herald* described these iron-nerved men as "classical heroes in the flesh, outwardly prosaic, incredibly nonchalant, crawling, climbing, walking, swinging, swooping on gigantic steel frames." This image also provides an excellent view of New York City street life, looking west on 34th Street with the 6th Avenue el and Macy's department store in the background.

Left: Ironworker and amateur photographer Charles Rivers, who packed a camera in his lunchbox, took this picture of himself at work bolting steel on the 52nd floor. Building engineers required each piece of structural steel to be placed at the specific point for which it had been engineered and milled. The reorganization in the methods used by the construction industry between 1900 and 1930 reflected the ideas that were being developed for the modern factory, such as the assembly line and the increased division of labor. Of the nearly 3,500 people working on the Empire State Building during the peak construction period in the summer of 1930, half were hired by subcontractors.

Above: A steelworker arranges a portion of the Empire State Building's frame in a Lewis Hine photo from 1930. In many respects, the advent of the great skyscrapers in the early twentieth century directly parallels the evolution of steel-frame construction, which, along with electrically powered elevators, enabled skyscrapers to rise in New York City and throughout the nation.

Below: As soon as a floor's concrete slab was completed, workers laid down narrow-gauge tracks, allowing materials to be moved around the site on flatcars. This rail was on the 85th floor.

Above: Workers lay concrete on the 6th floor setback. Because of the enormous amount of concrete needed to create the slabs, Empire State Building contractors prepared and mixed their own concrete on site.

Left: Men move a cart stacked with terra-cotta tiles into hoisting position. The tiles were used to fireproof the building's columns.

Below: Men strip away the wooden formwork from underneath a concrete slab. Wet concrete sets hard enough to support the weight of a man after about twenty-four hours. It takes another three to four days, however, before it can support its own weight.

Opposite: The skeleton of the Empire State Building consists of nearly fifty-seven thousand tons (51,699t) of steel. This weight, however, is not evenly distributed. The lower floors are larger in area and contain heavier columns than the upper floors. As a result, the top 40 percent of the building incorporates less than a quarter of the steel.

Below: This steelworker somehow manages to look relaxed, though he's just inches away from the edge of the beam. The beams on which these men worked were quite narrow and the heights were dizzying. Although six workers were killed during construction of the Empire State Building, this was considered an extremely good track record given the high degree of danger involved in almost every aspect of the work.

Above: Lewis Hine's great appreciation for the working man is evident in this portrait of a laborer.

Opposite and right: Over a span of six months, the fifty-five-year-old Hine took more than one thousand pictures of the construction workers. To get close-up shots, he often climbed on the steel frames himself. Particularly interested in the precarious interaction of man and machine, flesh and steel, he took photographs, including these two, that ennobled the laborers who braved the heights to earn their livings.

Above: As a decorative—though understated—touch, Swedish black granite is added to the 5th Avenue entrance of the Empire State Building. Most of the skyscraper's facade was made from limestone, a unique veneer in the 1930s.

Right: A construction worker lays a coat of fireproofing concrete onto the wind braces. These wind braces lent the Empire State Building its lateral strength.

Left: This photo of the lofty construction site, taken by Charles Rivers, shows the enormous expanse of steel that comprised the foundation of the building. Architects and builders viewed their primary challenge as maintaining a continuous flow of materials to the workers and ensuring that materials arrived at the site in a timely manner, especially with respect to the steel frames.

Left: Set against the Empire State Building's hulking steel frame, this worker looks very small, indeed. As New York's white-collar economy expanded in the 1920s, the demand for office spaced soared, prompting a surge in new construction throughout the city. After the stock market crashed, everything changed, and the skyscraper found itself struggling to attract tenants.

Below: A riveter strikes a lighthearted pose for photographer Lewis Hine. The newly completed Chrysler Building towers in the background.

Opposite: Al Smith liked to boast that all the labor on the Empire State Building was performed during regular business hours. This claim was rather disingenuous, however, since the "regular business hours" he referred to would begin at 3:30 A.M. and last until 4:30 P.M.—a thirteen-hour workday with only half an hour for lunch.

Above: This device was known as the Horton stone winch. Although much of the stone for the building could be raised to the correct elevation using a system of interior hoists and flatcars, the stone for the facade had to be lifted into position by exterior winches like this one.

Opposite: Laborer Harry Powers sits atop the highest beam in the skyscraper, seemingly indifferent to the precariousness of his perch. What looks frightening to us became second nature to the Empire State Building construction workers, who were predominantly Irish and Italian, but also included Greeks, Poles, and Native Americans from the Mohawk Nation. Unfortunately, as soon as the project was over, many of these men joined the legions of unemployed workers who struggled to keep their heads above water in Depression-era New York City.

Above and right: In order to maximize efficiency, all parts for the Empire State Building were prefabricated and customized to size prior to being assembled on site. Here, men work at various aspects of the assembly of the building's steel frame: above, a team of men position a column, and, at right, a laborer drives a bolt into a steel beam to attach it to the previously assembled structure.

HINE

Opposite: A worker directs the movement of materials on one of the building's interior hoists in a photograph by Lewis Wickes Hine.

Below: This view of construction workers on the 83rd floor puts the enormous scale of the building project in perspective.

Above: A view of the developing facade of the Empire State Building. Architect William F. Lamb considered himself a classic functionalist and eschewed any design flourishes that he felt were not in keeping with the practical needs of the building. The *New York Times* commented: "Men and women, boys and girls who have occasion to gaze daily at the splendid lines and massive structure of the Empire State Building will not easily reconcile themselves to architecture that is cheap or mean or even extravagantly whimsical."

Opposite: This photograph, likely taken from the Flatiron Building on 23rd Street, shows the nearly completed Empire State Building from the south, with Madison Square in the foreground.

Above: Masons maneuver into position the stone eagle columns that now flank the 5th Avenue building entrance. The padded ropes lead to a stone winch that supports the large block.

Opposite: The newly completed skyscraper seems shiny and new in this March 21, 1931, photograph.

Above: Workers put the finishing touches on the very top of the mooring mast—the intended docking point for dirigibles.

Left: Beaming with pride, construction workers raise the flag after the completion of the mooring mast.

Above: Never one to miss a photo opportunity, Al Smith poses in front of a replica of the building that was his pride and joy. Unfortunately for Smith, the completion of the Empire State Building may have been his last moment in the sun. His struggles throughout the 1930s to improve the building's desperate financial circumstances and his increasing estrangement from the national Democratic party, which now favored his adversary, Franklin D. Roosevelt, had taken their toll. By the end of that decade, the embittered politician had withdrawn from his earlier role as showman and chief publicist for the building.

Opposite: A crowd mills around the base of the Empire State Building, perhaps to admire the understated Art Deco details, such as the sleek, narrow windows and the subtle fanlike motifs.

Above: Al Smith tips his cap to the crowd at the formal opening of the Empire State Building—the crowning glory of his extraordinary rags-to-riches story. New York State Governor and future President Franklin D. Roosevelt participated in the festivities, and President Herbert Hoover pressed a button in Washington that turned on the radiant lights in the building's lobby.

CHAPTER THREE

If You Build It, Will They Come?

The entire week of the Empire State Building's opening in May 1931 was one of tremendous exhilaration. The gala celebration was presided over, with his usual aplomb, by Al Smith. Just as he and Raskob had hoped, in a city of multiple skyscrapers, one had captured the imagination of the people of New York City. The euphoria, however, was short-lived. The building desperately needed to attract tenants.

When the Empire State Building opened, its occupancy rate languished around a woeful 23 percent, even with Smith and Raskob pulling out all the stops to bring in their colleagues, friends, and friends of friends as tenants. Much to their chagrin, and to the consternation of H. Hamilton Weber, the new rental manager, six months after it was ready to be occupied, the gleaming, new building had acquired a pejorative nickname—the "Empty State Building."

Smith at first believed he could convince state agencies to move into the building. He soon realized, however, that his charm and powers of persuasion alone would not make them sign on the dotted line, nor did he have the necessary influence over Governor Roosevelt, with whom he had an increasingly frosty relationship. His luck was not discernibly better with commercial tenants— beyond signing on as tenants the building's contractors and suppliers, his own dentist, and Raskob's barber. It didn't take long for Weber to give up on finding exclusively long-term tenants; instead, he offered bargains on space rental for weeklong expositions and shows to groups such as the Real Estate Board of New York and the National Drapery Association.

Although advertising the space had begun in a relatively low-key manner, by 1932, Smith upped the ante by launching a massive public relations campaign. Engineered by Publicity Associates, a strategy was designed to keep the building in the public eye and to attract tenants by highlighting its stature in every conceivable manner. The promotional effort showcased the building (and Smith's relationship to it) in advertisements, press releases, newsreels, industry trade publications, educational newsletters, and magazine advertising columns. Undoubtedly, the campaign's most significant coup was the 1933 filming of the movie *King Kong*, which cast the Empire State Building in a starring role.

In 1934, Publicity Associates mailed more than thirty thousand folders—featuring color photographs of the sweeping views from the top of the building—to railroad ticket agents all over the country. The firm also arranged to have American Express clients provided with slips that entitled them to free trips to the observation deck. That same year, the *World Telegram* ran a story publicizing the building's

new restaurant, praising "Al Smith's stone and chromium nest" as the "coolest and most towering dinner and supper club in New York." In addition, having aired several special radio spots from the Empire State Building throughout the 1930s, in 1936 WOR began broadcasting a regular fifteen-minute radio show from the 86th-floor observation deck every afternoon except Sundays. The program, "Microphone in the Sky" starred the new general manager and press representative of the observation deck, Julia Chandler.

The Empire State Building was not only the first significant piece of real estate to use radio to promote itself; it also pioneered a brand new medium when the National Broadcasting Company leased the eastern half of the 85th floor for use as an experimental television and sound studio. Although it took time for NBC's television plans to bear fruit, its first antennas extended through the building's mooring mast and reached higher than anything in the city, finding a radical new use for the aborted dirigible tower.

Yet, despite the media fanfare, the popularity of *King Kong*, and the millions of dollars brought in by the observation deck, the restaurant, and the souvenir stands, the Empire State Building continued to hover near bankruptcy into the late 1930s. Smith declared 1936 the worst rental season in the city in three decades, and practically begged Metropolitan Life to cut its mortgage rate on the building in half so the owners could avoid defaulting on the loan. Met Life reduced its interest rate, but only after the owners paid an additional half a million dollars toward the principal. The most likely reason that Met Life didn't foreclose on the Empire State Building is that the mortgage company didn't want it either.

The former governor grew increasingly despondent. Frustrated by the economic depression and estranged from the Democratic administration of his adversary Franklin D. Roosevelt in Washington, Smith, who had taken such pride in showing off the building, cut back on his famous tours of the observation deck for foreign dignitaries. Just as with the rest of the city and the country, it would take a world war and its aftermath to make the Empire State Building solvent.

Opposite: One of New York City's halcyon moments in the twentieth century was the dedication ceremony for the Empire State Building on May 1, 1931. Here, a large crowd of dignitaries gathers in the front lobby of Al Smith's prized legacy for the grand celebration. Events in honor of the tallest skyscraper in the world would continue for a week, giving New Yorkers at least a short-term respite from the city's dismal economic news.

Right: The great skyscraper stands tall and proud upon completion in the 1930s. Despite all the accolades heaped on the building, the Great Depression nearly forced its owners into bankruptcy.

Above: From this vantage point, looking north over Central Park, the Empire State Building's steel-and-glass mooring mast appears to be massive, its shape mimicking that of the building as a whole.

Right: For many, the magnificent skyscraper at 34th Street and 5th Avenue stood as a symbol of boundless faith in New York City's ability to pull itself out of the Great Depression through the forces of commerce and capitalism.

Opposite: From 1938, one of the last photographs taken of Manhattan's elevated train lines shows the Empire State Building in the background. This el was used as a shuttle from 3rd Avenue to 2nd Avenue by the I.R.T. until it was rendered obsolete shortly afterwards.

Above: No, this is not some kind of weird fad. It is a view of the large crowd of people who observed a partial eclipse of the sun through protective film from the Empire State Building observation deck in August of 1932.

Opposite: The graceful pinnacle of the Empire State Building, shown here in March 1931, never functioned as a mooring mast, but was eventually put to good use as a radio and television tower.

Below: In one of two attempts to test the mooring mast, the dirigible *Columbia* tried to pick up bags of mail from the top of the building in September 1931 but was foiled by wind resistance and strong updrafts. Thousands of people watched the event from the street below.

Above: Although dirigibles were propeller driven and could be steered, they were even less stable than hot-air balloons and were always at the mercy of winds. Even before the *Columbia* experiment, Dr. Hugo Eckener, commander of the *Graf Zepplin*, noted: "The difficulties of mooring a great airship to a mast over New York City would be very great. The violent air currents up and down caused by your high buildings would, I think, make such a project almost impossible at this time."

Right: This sweeping 1931 view of Manhattan from the 27th floor of the River House apartment building on East 52nd Street showcases the landscape of Midtown Manhattan, transformed by the addition of the 1,250-foot (381m)-tall skyscraper earlier that year.

Above: A DC-4, the first Swedish passenger plane, flies up the East River on its way to La Guardia Airport in 1946, offering its passengers a spectacular view of the skyscrapers of Manhattan.

Above: From this angle it appears that this boy can reach out and touch the Empire State Building. In fact, he is enjoying the swings in St. Gabriel Park, which was located a few blocks south of the skyscraper, in August 1938.

Above: A view from the 69th floor of the RCA Building shows the skyscrapers of the New York skyline, which seem to be floating on a cloud on this foggy August day in 1943.

CHAPTER FOUR

The War Years

As early as January 1941, the Empire State Building's observation deck served as one of ten enemy-aircraft monitoring sites in the New York City metropolitan area. When the United States entered the war in December of that year, following the attack on Pearl Harbor, the outpost was staffed by volunteers who watched the skies around the clock and reported suspicious planes to Army Interceptor Command.

To serve the war effort, in January 1942, Mayor Fiorello La Guardia offered the federal government office space in the building at minimal cost—an offer that immediately reaped benefits when the regional bureau of the Office of Price Administration leased an astonishing five full floors with a whopping eighty thousand square feet (7,440m²) of office space. In 1942, Schenley Liquor became the top employer in the building when it signed a lease for five floors to house eight hundred employees. Al Smith later named John Hennessy, a former deputy chief inspector for the New York Police Department, as the building's coordinator of civilian defense. Hennessy conducted regular air raid drills and taught building tenants how to quickly respond and go to their safety stations. Because so many of the building's staff were on assignment in war factories, Smith made sure that safety precautions were stressed and were clearly understood by new personnel. It was the former governor's last official act. He died in the autumn of 1944.

The Empire State Building's prospects were looking up. Once regarded primarily as a tourist attraction, it was now hailed for having played a major role in aiding the national defense of the country. The building had supported the patriotic war effort by housing government agencies, had served as an antiaircraft advisory station, and had offered its observation deck to the service of the federal government. There was also a belief that the skyscraper could be a boon to the defense of the country in future conflicts.

Then, disaster struck. July 28, 1945, began as a typical, though particularly foggy, Saturday morning. Suddenly, at 9:49 A.M., there was a deafening explosion. An Army Air Corps B-25 bomber had smashed into the north wall of the Empire State Building, between the 78th and 79th floors, exploding on contact. Lieutenant Colonel William F. Smith, Jr., the plane's pilot, had been en route from Bedford, Massachusetts, and was attempting to land at Newark Airport when he severely miscalculated his flight path in the fog and ended up flying directly over Manhattan. When he finally dropped below the clouds, he discovered that he was surrounded by skyscrapers and heading right for the New York Central Building. He quickly banked to avoid that building, but his evasive action unfortunately put him on a course to collide with the Empire State Building. He had never flown a B-25 until two

Opposite: On the foggy Saturday morning of July 28, 1945, at 9:49 A.M., an Army Air Corps B-25 bomber on its way from Bedford, Massachusetts, to Newark Airport crashed into the north face of the Empire State Building, between the 78th and 79th floors. Fourteen people, including the pilot, were killed, and several dozen were injured, but most people were successfully evacuated. Surprisingly, the building sustained no serious structural damage.

days before the accident and it remains unclear to this day whether the accident was a result of pilot error or was caused either by plane malfunction or bad advice from the officials at La Guardia Airport, who had cleared Smith to land at Newark.

Thousands of terrified New Yorkers witnessed the explosion or heard the blast and assumed that the United States had been bombed. Colonel Smith was killed instantly, as were two other crew members and eleven people working at the National Catholic Welfare Conference, which had its office on the 79th floor. In retrospect, however, the results could have been much worse. Fortunately, the crash occurred on a weekend, rather than a normal business day, when there might have been as many as ten thousand tenants in the building. Since the nation was still in a state of war, emergency vehicles from the city's disaster unit responded immediately. Firefighters rushed to the site to douse the burning airplane fuel, and medical personnel soon arrived to tend to the injured. Perhaps the most amazing story was that of the miraculous survival of two elevator operators. The cable snapped on the elevator in which they were riding and the car plummeted to the subbasement. Thankfully, the emergency brakes slowed them down, and the two women were found alive.

Remarkably, despite major gashes in the southern and northern walls and the destruction of two full floors and a supporting steel post and beam, the structure itself sustained no permanent damage. Although the price tag for repair would be approximately $1 million, the building demonstrated its strength and resiliency. It was opened for business on all but the damaged floors the following Monday— just two days after the crash—and, soon after, people were again permitted to take in the view from the observation deck.

Equally astonishing, the falling debris did not injure anyone in any surrounding streets or buildings, though McCreery's department store across the street did file a claim for seven broken windows.

Within a month of the accident, the Army prohibited its planes from flying over New York City, except under special conditions. And three months after the crash, the Civil Aeronautics Administration (now the Federal Aviation Administration) set a policy requiring that private and commercial aircraft maintain a minimum altitude of 2,500 feet (762m) when flying over Midtown and Lower Manhattan.

Left: Fires rage on the top eleven floors of the Empire State Building as a result of the crash. Flaming fuel and one of the plane's tires landed on the roof of a nearby building, as evidenced here by the smoke in the foreground. At the time, as many as one hundred people were thought to have been injured in the crash. Fortunately, the number proved to be considerably lower. Mayor Fiorello La Guardia commented that if the plane had hit at an angle rather than striking head-on, the amount of falling debris could have been much greater, and the risk of death and injury much higher.

Opposite: Firefighters dig through the wreckage searching for the bodies of those who perished in the crash. Most of the victims were volunteers working for the War Relief Services of the National Catholic Welfare Conference, which was housed on the 79th floor. The agency aided thousands of individuals and families who had been rendered homeless or destitute by the war. In all, eleven young women who had come in that Saturday to help with paperwork were killed, as well as the pilot and two crew members.

Above: Firefighters solemnly sort through the debris in search of human remains. Most of the recovered bodies were badly burned, often making it difficult to identify them or even to distinguish between male and female victims. Searchers had to wade ankle-deep in water to conduct their rescue mission.

Opposite: Taken from a ledge on the 81st floor and looking down on 34th Street, this photograph presents a dizzying, bird's-eye view of the wreckage, which protrudes from an enormous gash in the north side of the building. The force of the impact sent pieces of the B-25 bomber careering through the 78th floor and out the south side of the building. One of the plane's engines ended up lodged in a fire escape. As it turned out, the pilot, Lieutenant Colonel William F. Smith, Jr., a decorated combat pilot and a graduate of West Point, had never flown a B-25 until the Thursday before the accident.

Above: In the immediate aftermath of the crash, New York City officials placed barricades at the corner of 34th Street and 5th Avenue to prevent people from being injured by falling debris. After measures had been taken to eliminate any danger to pedestrians and motorists, the barricades were removed. Here, concerned New Yorkers mill around the crash site, trying to get a glimpse of the damage.

Below: Harry Berger of the Bronx stands next to a section of the bomber plane that fell from the building after the crash. Following an investigation, tighter regulations were enacted to restrict low-flying aircraft between Midtown and Lower Manhattan.

Above: The day after the crash, the *New York Times* reported that the "Horror-stricken occupants of the building, alarmed by the roar of engines, ran to the windows just in time to see the plane loom out of the gray mists that swathed the upper floors of the world's tallest building.... It crashed with a terrifying impact along the north wall of the building." With the exception of one steel beam that was bent eighteen inches (45.5cm) upward by the sheer force of the plane's impact, the building's foundation successfully withstood the crash.

Below: Not surprisingly, the elevators above the floors where the crash occurred were knocked out of commission. In one close call, two elevator operators were stuck in elevator six when the cable snapped, sending them plummeting to the subbasement. Although the women suffered from burns and the shock they received from the impact of the fall, their injuries were minimal.

Below: Repairmen remove one of the ill-fated bomber's engines from the crash site. The Army probe into the crash prompted a major debate as to whether pilot error had caused the accident or Colonel Smith had received poor information from air traffic controllers at La Guardia Airport. The cause of the crash was never definitively determined.

Right: Firefighters logged an extraordinary number of hours dousing the fire, surveying the damage, and removing potential hazards. The building's fire alarms and emergency response mechanisms all functioned properly and promptly alerted authorities to the disaster.

Below: A firefighter pauses to examine a twisted girder during a damage survey on the 79th floor. With the exception of the observation decks and the floors that were damaged by fire, the Empire State Building was open for business the following Monday.

Opposite: Almost immediately after the tragic accident, workers began erecting scaffolding on the 33rd Street side of the Empire State Building to allow reconstruction work to take place on the two damaged floors.

Below: A large crowd of concerned onlookers flocked to the site the day after the crash to see—and document—the damage for themselves. Not surprisingly, New Yorkers were traumatized by the crash, and many believed their city was under attack.

Above: A 1969 photograph of the Manhattan skyline with the East River in the foreground. The Empire State and Chrysler Buildings are shrouded in the mist of a low cloud, which lends them a rather ethereal majesty.

CHAPTER FIVE

Preserving the Legacy

By the late 1940s, problems filling the Empire State Building with tenants were relegated to a memory of the Depression years. Business was thriving, as was tourism. The building became an early leader in the communications revolution when it erected a television antenna tower on top of the dirigible mooring dock, adding 225 feet (68.5m) to its height. By the mid-1950s, New York City's eight primary television stations were all transmitting their signals from atop the Empire State Building.

After Raskob's death in 1950, his family sold the building to a group of out-of-towners headed by Roger L. Stevens for $51 million. Stevens, who would later go on to head the Kennedy Center for the Performing Arts in Washington, D.C., became overwhelmed when the city increased its assessment on the building and, in 1954, he sold out to Illinois coal magnate Colonel Henry Crown. To promote the building, Crown sought out the services of public relations pioneer Benjamin Sonnenberg, who went to work immediately. His first initiative was "Operation: Light Up the Sky," or the "Freedom Lights." Installed at the foot of the television tower, four beacons of light, each measuring five feet (1.5m) in diameter, revolved 180 degrees per minute with perfect synchronization. This stunning display was the brightest continuous source of artificial light in the world.

In the 1950s, Crown and Sonnenberg also successfully enticed a variety of celebrities to the top of the building. Each visit—whether it was from Miss Universe or Queen Elizabeth—was turned into a major media event. *Time* magazine reported that the Empire State Building had become one of the world's most profitable buildings, grossing as much as $10 million a year and most likely netting nearly half that enormous sum. In 1956, the Voice of America produced a radio program called *From Tower to Tower*, which featured vocalists, actors, and others who performed and communicated from the world's four tallest television and radio towers: the Eiffel Tower, Berlin's radio tower, Stuttgart's television tower, and the Empire State Building.

In less than a decade, the value of the world-famous structure at 5th Avenue and 34th Street had soared to $65 million, the price paid by Empire State Associates—a company started by Lawrence Wien, with Harry Helmsley serving as his broker—when it purchased the building from Crown in 1961. An enormous demand for office space fueled a new construction boom in the 1950s that resulted in tenants filling a staggering 97 percent of the Empire State Building. Prominent new tenants during the Empire State Associates years included major banking and brokerage firms like Manufacturer's Hanover; Irving Trust; and Shearson, Hammill, and Reynolds.

Left: In September of 1950, a construction worker braves the vertiginous heights during the erection of the Empire State Building's television tower. Soon after the tower's completion, all the major New York–area stations moved their antennas to the top of the structure for maximum transmission.

The new owners promptly undertook a number of modernization projects: the facade was cleaned and the interior was fully refurbished. Air-conditioning was installed for 80 percent of the building and new, high-speed escalators were added to the lower floors. An "Introduction to New York" exhibit, designed to attract tourists on their way to the observation deck, was also created. One of Empire State Associates' less popular upgrades was the replacement of the original manually operated elevators with new push-button machines devoid of any human touch.

The 1964 New York World's Fair precipitated another change in the building. To kick off the event, the Freedom Lights were turned off and, in their place, the top thirty floors were illuminated by floodlights, resulting in a solid block of white light. The building's

Right: The new television antennas tower above the 86th floor observation deck in this image, circa 1950. Radio and television broadcasting created an enormous source of revenue for the skyscraper, far surpassing what the building would have brought in had the mooring mast idea proven to be practicable.

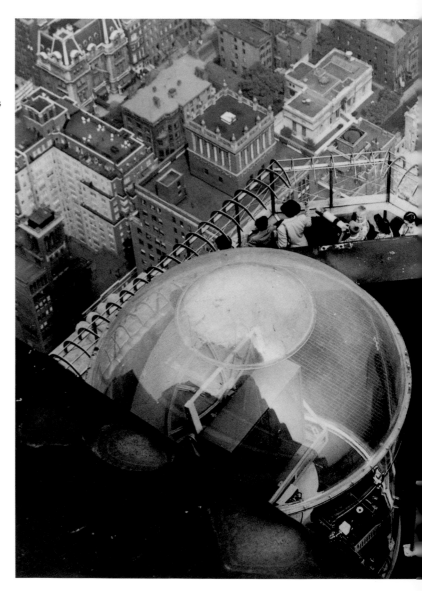

management sought to create a sleek, ultramodern lighting effect. Only a year later, however, the city and its proudest skyscraper were confronted with the blackout of 1965. During the power outage, a number of people in the Empire State Building found themselves stranded between floors in elevators until they could be rescued by firefighters. After this disturbing occurrence, the building owners made sure to create an emergency lighting system and a recall system for the elevators (a safety device that automatically lowers elevators to the next floor, where the doors can be opened manually) in case of a future blackout.

In the late 1960s, the Port Authority announced plans to construct a building in Lower Manhattan that would surpass the Empire State Building in height—it would be called the World Trade Center. The

Below: On Tuesday, November 9, 1965, at 5:30 P.M., New York City experienced a massive blackout. With all of Manhattan thrown into darkness, the two hundred people on the 86th floor observation deck enjoyed a magnificent view, illuminated only by the full moon and the stars.

plan was met with bitter opposition from Wien and his publicity agent, Robert Kopple. They were not only reluctant to lose the right to the moniker "the world's tallest building," but also feared that the new twin towers would glut the real estate market with office space, which would be filled at the expense of the Empire State Building and other privately owned and operated structures. One architect, Robert Jones, even proposed tearing down the Empire State's mooring mast and its top six stories and replacing them with a new thirty-three-story structure that would make the building 144 feet (44m) higher than the World Trade Center and 44 feet (13.5m) higher than the proposed Sears Tower in Chicago. Most prominent architectural critics hated Jones's idea, and a 1972 editorial in the *New York Times* declared that "the [Empire State] building's characteristic silhouette stands for the city of New York almost uniquely. Its Art Deco tower is not just the most important local landmark, it is also an undisputed artistic monument of international stature." Jones's idea was dead on arrival.

Above: Even before the "Freedom Lights" were inaugurated in the 1950s, the building used unique lighting touches to honor special dates. Here a dim-out of the structure honors Thomas Edison's birthday.

Right: In the 1950s and 1960s, the Empire State Building received a large number of foreign dignitaries. In October 1957, Queen Elizabeth II and Prince Phillip visited the observation deck. The Queen, clad in a fur stole, declared the view "the most beautiful thing I've ever seen." Standing next to the couple is Richard Patterson, the official City Greeter. To the Queen's left is building owner Henry Crown and his wife, and next to them is Willy Buchanan, State Department Chief of Protocol. Her Majesty was later presented with a gold-plated model of the building from Tiffany's.

It didn't take long for the Empire State Building's public relations department to recoup in the 1970s and 1980s. The skyscraper built in 1930 may not have been the world's tallest anymore, but it was now touted as the "world's most famous," and visitors continued to flock in huge numbers to its observation deck. In 1976, the year of the U.S. Bicentennial, the Empire State Building received its fifty-millionth visitor, and Wien and Helmsley changed the Empire State's lighting scheme at the request of the city's Convention and Bicentennial Commission. The white floodlights were replaced with patriotic red, white, and blue lights.

Thus began the tradition of changing the color of the Empire
State Building's lights to commemorate various holidays: green for
St. Patrick's Day; red and white for Valentine's Day; red, white, and
green for Columbus Day; and red, black, and green for Martin Luther
King Jr.'s birthday. The colors gracing the top of the building also
reflected local and national events. When the Yankees won the 1977
World Series, the building flashed blue and white lights; after the
1979 Camp David Accords, two sides of the building were lighted
in the state colors of Israel and the other two in the state colors of
Egypt. Although not all observers were enamored with the changes

in the lighting policy, it made the building more popular than ever
with tourists and Empire State Building tenants. By the early 1980s,
only a little more than twenty thousand square feet (1,860m²) of
space was vacant—an occupancy rate of nearly 99 percent.

In 1983, the Empire State Building celebrated its fiftieth anniversary. Architecture critic Paul Goldberger affirmed the meaning of the
legendary skyscraper in an article in the *New York Times*: "[It is]
about height, it is about commerce, it is about entertainment, it is
about views, it is about the very meaning of the skyline itself." Eight
years later, Peter Malkin took control of Empire State Associates and
the Prudential Life Insurance Company sold the land, which it had
purchased from Crown in 1961, to a group led by Donald Trump and
the family of Japanese tycoon and notorious organized crime figure
Hideki Yokoi. Although Trump attempted to evict Malkin and
Helmsley and break the master lease in 1994, a New York State
Supreme Court judge granted a temporary injunction, and the two
men maintained the lease on the building.

Throughout the 1990s, the city of New York provided the Empire
State Building with a $65 million modernization plan that included
upgrades to the fire and security systems and all-new windows and
window frames. Even during the recession in the early 1990s, the
occupancy rate hovered near 95 percent and the observation deck
continued to attract upwards of two million visitors each year. The
building won new awards for management and historical preservation.

After the devastating terrorist attacks destroyed the twin towers
of the World Trade Center on September 11, 2001, killing thousands
who were trapped inside, Empire State Building occupants undoubtedly
confronted acute fears. Could they be next? On October 4, 2001, less
than a month after the attacks, Malkin made a bid to purchase the
Empire State Building outright from Trump State Partners for $57.5
million, and in the spring of 2002, Trump agreed to sell. At the same
time, Malkin sought to allay the fears of tenants and visitors by
installing metal detectors and x-ray scanning machines in the lobby.

Today, in the post–September 11 climate, New Yorkers and
tourists alike appreciate this extraordinary structure as never before.
Since the Empire State Building once again became the tallest skyscraper in New York, visitors have packed its observation deck to
take in its world-famous view. At a time of collective mourning and
defiance, the Art Deco skyscraper, built in less than two years during
the Great Depression, seems to stand even taller as a symbol of the
city's resilience and strength.

Left: One observer noted that before the Empire State Building was constructed, there were many skyscrapers in New York City, but after the massive structure on 34th Street and 5th Avenue was completed, there was only one.

Opposite: These sightseers were caught unawares by an updraft on the building's observation deck. By 1954, when this photograph was taken, the Empire State Building had established itself as a major moneymaker in terms of attracting both tourists and tenants.

Above: From *An Affair to Remember* to *Sleepless in Seattle*, the Empire State Building has long been considered a romantic spot for couples in love.

Opposite: in 1983, for the fiftieth anniversary celebration of the original *King Kong* movie, an eighty-foot (24.5m)-tall balloon replica of the great ape was tied to the mooring mast as part of a publicity stunt put on by a company that manufactured giant inflatable advertising displays. The wind, however, was too much for the beast and gusts soon tore a hole through the balloon, which deflated and had to be taken down.

Right: No matter who you are, the opportunity to be photographed in front of the Empire State Building means that you have truly arrived in New York City. Here, a troupe of elephants and a zebra amble down 33rd Street to publicize the arrival of the famous Ringling Bros. and Barnum & Bailey Circus. If P.T. Barnum had been alive, he would no doubt have stood front and center with the animals.

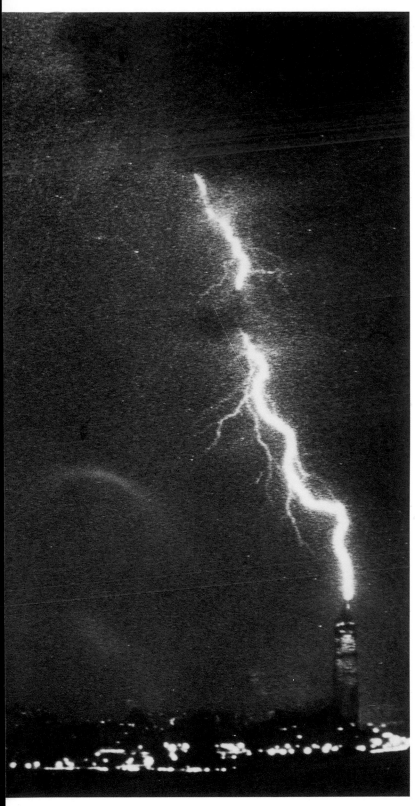

Left: Bolts of lightning create a spectacular display as they simultaneously strike the Empire State Building and the World Trade Center in this photograph taken from New Jersey. Designed to act as a lightning rod, the Empire State Building is struck more than one hundred times each year. When lightning strikes the top, the energy is channeled throughout the steel structure and, eventually, safely into the ground.

Above: Soldiers marvel at the breathtaking view from the heights of the Empire State Building's observation deck in 1949.

Left: The setbacks of the Empire State Building add enormously to its character. They not only create interesting patterns of light and shadow on the facade, but also emphasize the sweeping height of the tower.

Below: In the post–World War II era, the Empire State Building's publicist, Ben Sonnenberg, conceived of a spectacular light display called the "Freedom Lights," which consisted of four beacons that rotated in perfect synchronization. It was said that they could be seen from as far away as three hundred miles (483km) by air and eighty miles (129km) from the ground. Here, workers place one of the new beacon lights in position on the building's 90th floor.

Right: This stunning image was captured on April 11, 1956, when the new "Freedom Lights" atop the Empire State Building were turned on for the first time. The beacons were built at a cost of $500,000 and concentrated almost two billion candelas of light—the brightest continuous source of artificial light in the world.

Above: The Empire State Building forms the majestic centerpiece of the Manhattan cityscape in this 1955 photograph.

Sources

BOOKS

Burns, Ric, et al., *New York: An Illustrated History*. New York: Knopf, 1999.

Tauranac, John A., *The Empire State Building: The Making of a Landmark*. New York: Scribner, 1995.

Willis, Carol ed., *Building the Empire State*. New York and London: W.W. Norton and Company, 1998.

Whyte, William H. *The W.P.A. Guide to New York City*. New York: New Press, 1995. (Originally published 1939).

WEBSITES

ABCNews.com. "1945 Plane Crash Rocked NYC." http://abcnews.go.com/sections/us/DailyNews/WTC_planecrash_empirestate010911.html

CNNmoney. "Bid for Empire State," (October 4, 2001). http://money.cnn.com/2001/10/04/news/empire_state/index.htm

Daniel's Manhattan Architecture. http://users.commkey.net/daniel/empire.htm

Empire State Building: Official Internet Site. www.esbnyc.com

Fare, Phil. Art Deco. http://orathost.cfa.ilstu.edu/exhibits/pcfare/deco.html

Matthews, Kevin, ed. and Artifice, Inc. Great Buildings Online. www.greatbuildings.com/buildings/Empire_State_Building.html

NewYork.com. www.newyork.com/visit/attractions/empire_state_building.html

Robins, Tony. Art Deco Metropolis: The Whiz-Bang Buildings of Modern New York. http://www.pipeline.com/~trob/artdeco1.htm

Troncale, Anthony T. New York Public Library Miriam and Ira Wallach Division of Art, Prints, and Photographs: Photography Collection. www.nypl.org/research/chss/spe/art/photo/hinex/empire/empire.html

Wright, Leigh Martinez. "Spiders in the Sky," Smithsonian Magazine (January 2002). www.smithsonianmag.si.edu/smithsonian/issues02/jan02/indelible.html

Above: Bertram Brandt, a staff photographer at Acme Newspictures, took several photographs of the Empire State Building from the windows of his 16th-floor office in 1949. Here, looking due east, he captures the skyscraper glowing under a clear, mid-November night sky. Macy's department store is visible to the left and the McAlpin Hotel stands just to the right of the world's most famous skyscraper.

Photo Credits

AP/Wide World: pp. 2–3, 77, 78, 79 left, 79 right, 84–85, 87, 89, 90, 91, 97 bottom, 102–103, 106, 107, 108–109, 116, 118–119.

Brown Brothers: pp. 16, 17, 18–19, 28, 61 right, 63, 64, 67, 88, 94 left, 94–95, 111, 112–113.

Corbis: pp. 13 top, 32–33, 40, 41, 44, 48, 50, 51, 57 bottom, 66, 68–69, 70, 72–73, 74 top, 75, 76, 80–81, 83, 92, 93, 96, 97 top, 98, 99, 100–101, 114 left, 114–115, 117, 120, 121, 122 left, 122–123, 126.

Hulton/Archive: pp. 20-21, 82, 124–125.

Museum of the City of New York, www.mcny.org: pp. 8–9, 13 bottom (Gift of Carleton G. Maclean), 22 (Gift of Joseph J. Nardone), 23, 59, 61 left, 74 bottom, 104–105; ©Dwight Franklin: pp. 58 left, 58 right; ©Lewis Hine, Permanent Deposit of the Empire State Building: pp. 6–7, 29, 38–39, 49, 54–55, 56, 60; ©Robert A. Knudtsen, Gift of the Photographer: pp. 14–15; ©Beecher Ogden: p.12; ©Charles Rivers, Gift of the Photographer: pp. 42 bottom, 43, 47, 53; Shreve, Lamb and Harmon, Gift of the Architects: pp. 10, 31.

Skyscraper Museum, www.skyscraper.org: pp. 24, 25, 26, 27, 30, 34, 36, 37 top, 37 bottom, 42 top, 45 left, 45 right, 46 top, 46 bottom, 52 top, 52 bottom, 57 top, 62, 65 top, 65 bottom.

Index